WILD BIRD GUIDES

Great Horned Owl

WILD BIRD GUIDES

Great Horned Owl

Dwight G. Smith

STACKPOLE
BOOKS

Published by
STACKPOLE BOOKS
5067 Ritter Road
Mechanicsburg, PA 17055
www.stackpolebooks.com

Printed in China

10 9 8 7 6 5 4 3 2 1

First edition

Cover photo by Dr. Wayne Lynch and Aubrey Lang
Cover design by Tracy Patterson

Library of Congress Cataloging-in-Publication Data

Smith, Dwight G.
    Great horned owl / Dwight G. Smith
       p.   cm. — (Wild bird guides)
    Includes bibliographical references (p.).
    ISBN 0-8117-2689-4
    1. Great horned owl. I. Title. II. Series
QL696.S83 S57   2002   2002020204
598.9'7—dc21

Contents

An All-American Owl

Like the Americans with which it begrudgingly shares the landscape of two continents, the Great Horned Owl is a complex mix of personalities. By nature, it is a shy and solitary owl of rugged and remote locations, shunning both daylight hours and developed habitats of human landscapes. As a predator, it is a savage and sanguine opportunist equipped to take almost any small or medium-size animal, from grasshopper to grouse, for food with equal facility. Yet during courtship, this powerful owl transforms into a sometimes bashful though at other times exuberant pursuer of the opposite sex. Mated pairs are both boisterous and aggressive in proclaiming and defending their territory and even more fierce and formidable in defense of the nest and young. This same owl is exceptionally tender and solicitous in its loving devotion to its young.

The Great Horned Owl is the dominant bird of prey, or raptor, of the night. It is the nocturnal equal of the Golden Eagle in the West and the Red-tailed and Red-shouldered Hawks in the East.

Although both the Snowy Owl and Great Gray Owl are larger in size, they are not equal to the Great Horned Owl in weight, power, or aggressiveness. During the nocturnal hours, the Great Horned Owl, which well deserves its reputation for strength and savagery, is the undisputed king of its domain. Though a few of our owls are larger, and the smaller owls may be faster or more agile, none of them dispute the landscape with the Great Horned Owl.

Adaptive, cunning, and opportunistic, the Great Horned Owl occurs in almost all North American landscapes, from tundra to desert. Bold and beautiful to behold, this owl, more than any other, is both the spirit and the symbol of wild America. It is truly an all-American owl, occurring from the high tundra of Alaska and Canada southward to the Straits of Magellan and on into Patagonia and points south. Its range is from at least 68 degrees north latitude, in the Yukon Territory in the West and Labrador in the East, to 54 degrees south in Tierra del Fuego. It is absent only from some of the smaller offshore islands of the Pacific Northwest, the West Indies, and the lowland rain forests of Central America and Amazonia.

Throughout its range, the Great Horned Owl occurs within an enormous variety of climatic conditions. It breeds under temperature and moisture extremes varying from the summer heat and dryness of the Sonoran and Chihuahuan Deserts to extended periods of freezing temperatures along the northern limits of its range at the edge of the boreal forest. Although this owl can endure extended periods of snow and ice cover, it is probably less adapted, physiologically, to cold and snow than the Snowy and Great Gray Owls.

The Great Horned Owl occupies a wide assortment of habitats. Although once considered primarily an owl of interior forests, the great horned is actually more common in the mosaic of fields and woodlands throughout both northern and southern temperate regions of its range. It is less common in deeper woods, pygmy woodlands, chaparral, tall grasslands, semiarid grasslands, shrub-steppe communities, and desert, although it is often ecologically important as the top carnivore within these habitats as well. A detailed list of Great Horned Owl habitats would include woodlands of all types, swamps and mangroves, fresh- and saltwater marshes, prairie, semiarid grasslands, sagebrush, mesquite, paloverde, and cacti deserts, suburbs, and cities. In Latin America, its many habitats include lowland tropical and subtropical rain forests, cloud forests, second-growth forests, coffee plantations, pastures, and clear-cut areas in rain forests.

Great Horned Owls are typically absent only from the treeless far north, the alpine meadows of high mountainous areas, and the most heavily urbanized landscapes. Even in these areas, however, they may occasionally foray in search of food. As pairs and individuals have become increasingly tolerant of or at least behaviorally more adept at living in human-modified landscapes, more and more owls are taking up residency in the orchardlike habitats of suburbia, along tree-lined greenbelts and greenways of cities, and in the larger cemeteries and parks. A few enterprising pairs have nested in city cemeteries and other urban open space, although not always successfully.

The name Great Horned Owl reflects the bird's size, strength, and large ear tufts. Throughout its extensive range, it has many nicknames, including hoot owl, cat owl, tiger owl, and sometimes the evil owl, because of the superstitions and folklore surrounding it. The French call it the *Grand-duc d'Amerique* (the "great American owl"), while to the Spanish it is *Buho Americano,* which roughly translates as "American hoot owl."

Along with all of the other owls, the Great Horned Owl belongs to the avian order Strigiformes. The 205 species of owls all have a rounded facial disk, forward-directed eyes that give them binocular vision, and soft feathers for silent flight. They are a widespread and successful group of birds occupying virtually all habitats on all continents, from tundra to tropics. All are nocturnal, or nearly so, and most feed primarily on small mammals. A few species, including the Great Horned Owl, extend their activity periods into twilight and sometimes into daylight hours and, consequently, often have a more varied diet.

Two distinct families of owls are recognized. The family Tytonidae includes 16 species of barn, grass, and bay owls, which have a distinctive monkeylike face, a pronounced heart-shaped facial disk, small eyes, a comblike middle toe, and a tail in which the outer feathers are longer than the central feathers. The other 189 species, including the Great Horned Owl, are loosely grouped in the family Strigidae. This family lacks the "monkey face," but all have a more or less pronounced facial disk, large, wide-set eyes, and a tail in which the central feathers are the longest.

Ancestrally, the Great Horned Owl *(Bubo virginianus)* probably derived from a Eurasian horned owl that arrived in North America sometime during the early or mid-Pleistocene, most likely via the Bering Sea land bridge, and then dispersed down along the ice-free corridor west of the northern glaciers. Their dispersal southward and across the continent was probably swift, as there apparently were no ecological equivalents of these large owls at that time in the New World. Fossil evidence suggests that the early representatives of horned owls in North America were considerably larger than today's species, more closely resembling the huge Eurasian Eagle Owl *(Bubo bubo),* left, which is about 40 percent larger than the largest subspecies of Great Horned Owl. For example, fossils of *Bubo sinclairi,* an early Great Horned Owl found in caves in Northern California from the Upper Pleistocene, are somewhat larger than the modern species. Owl ornithologist Karl Voous suggests that there has been a slow but continuous decrease in Great Horned Owl size corresponding to the elimination or at least the decrease of medium-size and larger prey in many areas of its range, especially in the more settled regions of both continents.

Today the Great Horned Owl is the only New World representative of the large group of eagle owls of the Old World, although some owl biologists believe that the southernmost subspecies, *B. v. magellanicus,* is a separate species of horned owl because it is considerably smaller and vocally distinct.

The Great Horned Owl's Old World relatives include a dozen species of eagle owls and fish owls, all belonging to the genus *Bubo.* The *Bubo* owls are a widespread and successful genus of large, horned owls that occur throughout much of Eurasia and Africa, ranging from the woodland limits in the north of Eurasia south through Europe, Asia, the Middle East, and into much of Africa south of the Sahara. They are absent only from Australia and some of the Pacific Islands. Like the Great Horned Owl, the eagle owls occupy virtually every type of ecological habitat found in the Old World, except tundra and alpine areas, as well as humid lowland forests of Central Africa and Southeast Asia.

In the field, the Great Horned Owl is unmistakable. It is the only large, heavy owl with prominent ear tufts that superficially resemble ears. Male and female are similar in coloration and cannot be told apart in the field, although the female is larger and heavier.

Plumage colors are mostly earth shades that help conceal the bird in its daylight roosts. Its overall coloring is a basic undertone of white to buff, densely spotted or mottled with various shades of brown or tawny. The underparts of the belly and breast have brown or tawny barring, and the feathers are tipped with dark brown or black. A pure white or orange-buff throat bib is evident when the bird is perched. The legs are fully feathered in various shades and mottling of brown or buff. The short tail is edged with white and crossed

with six or seven bands. The large eyes vary from bright yellow to a lemon chrome yellow. The face is dull tawny or dingy ocher, with white eyebrows. It is ornamented by the rather large ear tufts, which have black outer webs and ocher inner webs. A slate or blackish bill is partly hidden in the facial feathers.

In flight, the Great Horned Owl shows densely barred underwings of buff or brown. The ear tufts fall back against the rounded head, and it resembles a buteo hawk with a short tail, but its flight is more purposeful, with powerful wingbeats.

As might be expected of a species that occupies two continents and several dozen ecological habitats, the different subspecies show somewhat different color patterns. Woodland races are usually darker, with a tawny orange face, and more heavily mottled and barred, both on the back and below, while desert and semiarid owls tend to be grayer with a rusty face. Great Horned Owls of the northern and northwestern woodlands are larger and paler, with the face and body a grayish that increasingly resembles the plumage color of immature Snowy Owls. The southernmost subspecies, the Magellanic Horned Owl, is small, light, and finely barred. Its size and color differences are thought by some owl taxonomists to be sufficiently different to warrant its being considered a separate New World species.

By every measure, the Great Horned Owl is one of the most successful of all New World species of owls. It owes its success chiefly to a combination of morphology and behavior, which admirably shapes it for the role of nocturnal predator. Its basic physical characteristics include a large, barrel-shaped body; broad, rounded wings that provide maneuverability for negotiating through woodlands in search of prey or to and from the nest site, as well as the power needed to lift jackrabbits and other relatively heavy prey; powerful feet equipped with sharp talons for catching and killing prey; and a large, raptorial bill for tearing flesh and bones.

As with all owls, the feathers of a great horned are soft-edged for silent flight. The comblike fringes of the leading edge, the slimmer part of the feather to the left of the midrib, or rachis, channel air over the wing, thereby reducing friction. The longer fringes of the trailing edge similarly reduce turbulence, and therefore noise, where the air streams flowing over and under the wing surface meet. The fuzzy softness of the upper surface minimizes friction between adjacent feathers during the up and down motions of each wingbeat. The silent flight resulting from these feather modifications conceals the owl on its approach while simultaneously permitting the bird to listen for any movement of the prey.

The feathers also provide effective layers of insulation that allow this owl to inhabit landscapes as diverse as boreal forests and tropical rain forests, while also permitting the stealthy approach needed by this nocturnal predator. The owls constantly preen their feathers, drawing the ends through their mandibles.

In the field, the Great Horned Owl's size conveys an impression of power and strength. The bird is formidably huge, averaging 22 to 23 inches (56 to 59 centimeters) in length, with a wingspan approaching 44 to 55 inches (112 to 140 centimeters). It is also one of the heaviest American owls, with females of the nominate subspecies *B. v. virginianus* averaging nearly 4 pounds (1,750 grams) and males about 2.9 pounds (1,300 grams), or about 15 percent less than females. Subspecies occurring along the more southern parts of North America, such as *B. v. pallescens,* are considerably lighter, with males averaging slightly over 2 pounds (900 grams) and females 2.5 pounds (1,140 grams).

The Great Horned Owl is exceeded in size by the Great Gray Owl *(Strix nebulosa)* and Snowy Owl *(Nyctea scandiaca)*. The Great Gray Owl (at left) of boreal forests, bogs, and northern swamps is spectacularly large, with a length of 27 inches (69 centimeters) and wingspan of 52 inches (132 centimeters). Much of its apparent bulk, however, consists of multiple layers of feathers, as its average weight is 2.4 pounds (1,080 grams), considerably lighter than the Great Horned Owl. In the field, the great gray is readily distinguished by its large, rounded head and smallish eyes set in a heavily ringed facial disk.

The Snowy Owl is a large white owl of the arctic tundra. Males are nearly pure white, but females are variously speckled with brownish spots and bars. Also called the White Owl, the Snowy Owl averages 23 inches (58 centimeters) in length and 52 inches (132 centimeters) in wingspan. With an average weight of about 4 pounds (1,830 grams), Snowy Owls are somewhat heavier than Great Horned Owls. The two species rarely overlap in either habitat use or prey selection, except when Snowy Owls are driven southward by drastic declines of lemmings, which are their dietary staple and also their main prey species.

The only other North American owl with prominent ear tufts is the Long-eared Owl *(Asio otus)*. This crow-size owl of woodland and edge habitats is a smaller and slimmer version of the Great Horned Owl, averaging about 15 inches (38 centimeters) in length, 36 inches (91 centimeters) in wingspan, and about half a pound (227 grams) in weight. It is buff or tawny, boldly streaked and barred with brownish or brownish black. The Long-eared Owl's ear tufts are close-set above a somewhat rusty orange facial disk surrounding small, yellow eyes.

Several species of screech owls also have ear tufts, but they are all considerably smaller than the Great Horned Owl, generally averaging about 7 to 9 inches (18 to 22 centimeters) in length, 20 to 24 inches (51 to 61 centimeters) in wingspan, and about half a pound (227 grams) or less in weight. The three North American screech owls, the Eastern Screech Owl *(Otus asio)*, Western Screech Owl *(Otus kennicotti)*, and Whiskered Screech Owl *(Otus trichopsis)*, are barely larger than a jay, and their ear tufts are less than an inch in length. Both Western and Whiskered Screech Owls are grayish; the Eastern Screech Owl has three color morphs—red, gray, and an intermediate chocolate.

The Barred Owl *(Strix varia)* and Spotted Owl *(Strix occidentalis)*, along with their Latin American kin, represent another group of woodland and wetland owls that occasionally overlap in habitat and home range with Great Horned Owls. The Barred Owl (shown here), however, prefers thick coniferous woods, river forests, and wooded wetlands, while the Spotted Owl is a western bird of old-growth humid forests and coniferous woodlands. Both are medium-size, dark brown owls. In the field, these owls can be distinguished from the Great Horned Owl by their lack of ear tufts, rounded facial disks, and dark eyes.

Owls have long been the focus of innumerable fables and folklore, and much superstition surrounds them. On one hand, the owl was considered a companion of witches and sorcerers of the night, a harbinger of evil or ill tidings, or a bird of trickery. On the other hand, it was admired for its strength, courage, and stealth.

Because owls often roost in deserted buildings and utter eerie, almost humanlike cries, shrieks, and screams, early peoples ascribed all kinds of weird attributes to these strange birds of the night. They thought owls were the nocturnal companions of witches and wizards and attached ominous signs and portents to their ghostly calls—if someone heard the cry of an owl during the night, some disaster or death was sure to follow.

The early colonials readily attached Old World fables and folklore to the great horned and other North American owls, and they added a few new legends as well. In the South, for example, the cry of a Great Horned Owl was thought to forecast the immediate future: If an owl hooted on one's right side, good luck was sure to follow, but if it hooted on one's left, the person was in for a spell of misfortune.

Native Americans had various local tribal legends. Some northwestern tribes believed that the owl was the Evil One, who during the night called out the names of men and women marked for death. Other tribes thought the owl was a winged Satan who had been exiled from the daytime world of the sun. The Pueblo Indians called it the Skeleton Man, which they equated with the god of death. To the Sioux Hin-han, the owl was the guardian of the Milky Way, who inspected the spirits of the dead; those lacking the proper tattoo on their wrists were forever barred from entering the realms of the stars and thrown into a bottomless abyss.

Warriors of many tribes admired the strength, courage, and beauty of the Great Horned Owl above all other owls. Some tribes even revered the big owls in ceremonial functions. The Pimi of the Southwest believed that owls represented the spirits of departed warriors, which assumed the shape of the birds and restlessly wandered about through the night. The Arikara of the Great Plains had mystic owl societies in which initiates were adorned with facial masks of the wing and tail feathers of Great Horned Owls. Some Indian nations held the owl in high esteem as a friendly spirit who gave both warnings and advice, as needed. The Passama-quoddy of the Maine woods credited the owl with magical powers of love and thought its song in the night was a magic love flute. The Hopi of the Southwest associated the Great Horned Owl with fertility of a different sort, believing that the summer calling of the owl brought hot weather, which produced a good peach crop.

During their ceremonies marking the winter solstice, the Hopi used owl feathers to help summon the return of summer and its heat. A number of Indian tribes employed the Great Horned Owl's feathers for more practical uses. The Indians of northern New Mexico fletched their arrows with the feathers to make them fly silently toward their targets. The Zuni held owl feathers in their mouth, hoping that this would cause them to stalk game as quietly as the owl flies.

An Iroquois legend explained how the Great Horned Owl was formed. Raweno, the Everything-Maker, was busy shaping all of the animals as unformed Owl looked down from a branch. Everything-Maker was shaping the hind legs of Rabbit when Owl interrupted, saying, "I want you to make me the most beautiful, the fastest, and the most wonderful of all birds." Everything-Maker told Owl to be quiet and wait his turn, but obstinate Owl replied, "Whoo whoo, nobody can forbid me to watch." This annoyed Everything-Maker. He pulled Owl down from his branch and stuffed his head deep into his body, making his ears stick out, and his eyes grew wide with fright. "There," said Everything-Maker. "Now you will have big ears to hear me and big eyes so you won't have to crane your neck around to watch things you shouldn't watch." After he finished shaping Owl, Everything-Maker rubbed mud all over him instead of giving him bright colors. When he was satisfied, Everything-Maker said, "Since I work during the day, you will be awake only at night." Great Horned Owl flew off pouting, "Whoo whooo." And that is why the Great Horned Owl has such big eyes and big ears and only comes out at night. As for Rabbit, he was so afraid that he ran off before Everything-Maker could finish shaping him. That is why his hind legs are so much longer than his front legs. Even to this day, Rabbit is timid and afraid of just about everything.

A Ruthless and Efficient Hunter

To the early naturalists, the Great Horned Owl was a savage and sanguine hunter, an ample and powerful provider of food for its mate and its young. Ecologists prefer to classify this huge owl as a generalist and opportunistic predator able to exploit an exceptionally wide food base. Both descriptions are reasonably accurate and merge together into a picture of a powerful and dominant nocturnal hunter of great strength, hunting skill, and diet versatility. All small and medium-size animals that fly, crawl, walk, run, swim, or burrow are its potential foods, and none of them dare to move about at night except in constant fear and timidity.

Like all predators, the Great Horned Owl is closely tied to its food supply, which in turn directly dictates its fate, survival, and reproduction. Sharp seasonal differences in prey abundance and availability can spell disaster or death or mass movements out of areas where food is lacking; declines in snowshoe hare populations lead to mass movements of Great Horned Owls southward in search of food.

Natality is also closely linked to availability of food for these big owls. A number of studies, including my study of nesting ecology in central Utah, have convincingly demonstrated that nesting success and productivity (number of young produced) of these and other large raptors strongly track their food supply. In good prey years, more pairs of Great Horned Owls nest earlier in the season, produce larger clutches of eggs, and successfully fledge more young. Furthermore, the fledged young show much higher survival rates through fall and winter. In poor prey years, however, productivity declines; nesting begins later in the season, the owls lay smaller clutches, and success of the young both in the nest and as fledglings declines or becomes increasingly marginal. In very low prey years, many pairs may not nest at all.

For all Great Horned Owls, food supply is a daily—as well as seasonal—concern. Every day of every season, a central and critical theme in the nocturnal life of every Great Horned Owl is the need to find food. The bird must be able to find and identify suitable prey, stalk and strike it, kill and dismember or otherwise prepare the food, and consume it. Under extreme circumstances, a Great Horned Owl may endure several days without food, but then it must find food in order to survive. Metabolic studies suggest that an average-size Great Horned Owl requires from 50 to 100 grams of food per day. This daily food requirement may be met by a few meadow mice, deer mice, shrews, or songbirds. A single large prey item, such as a ground squirrel, woodchuck, grouse, or duck, may supply food for several days.

Although individual Great Horned Owls may sometimes feed on fresh carrion, especially in winter months or during times of low food availability, the majority of their food consists of live animals that they must hunt down and kill.

Like all owls, the Great Horned Owl is superbly equipped for the seemingly difficult role of a nocturnal hunter. It uses a combination of large eyes, excellent hearing, and silent flight to target suitably-sized prey. The tubular eyes of Great Horned Owls are exceptionally large and set in bony sockets that greatly restrict eye movement. In order to see from one side to another, the owl must turn its head. To compensate for the relative immobility of its eyes, the Great Horned Owl's neck has flexible cervical vertebrae that permit it to turn its head over 180 degrees, thereby enabling the owl to look almost directly behind it without moving its body.

The eyes of owls are also unique among birds in that they face forward, giving them binocular vision similar to that of humans. The wide-set eyes have large corneal surfaces and large lenses for light gathering. Both their size and position are adaptive for nocturnal hunting. The large eyes are densely packed with light-gathering rods that help the owl detect prey under very low-light conditions, and the overlapping fields resulting from binocular vision allow the Great Horned Owl to better judge the distance to prey. This and other owls make head-bobbing movements when watching potential prey, which undoubtedly helps the birds estimate distance to moving or stationary animals.

The Great Horned Owl's extra-
ordinary vision is supplemented
by excellent auditory capabilities.
The "horns" or feather tufts of
the Great Horned Owl, while
sometimes mistakenly called
ears, actually function only as
recognition features. Its real ears
are hidden within the feathers
on the sides of the head. During
evening or early-morning hunts,
the bird uses both its eyes and
ears to locate and target suitable
prey. On moonless nights, however, it relies more and more
on its exceptional hearing ability.
When a Great Horned Owl hears
the movements of potential prey,
it turns its head toward the
sound, using the facial disk of
flattened feathers to direct and
amplify faint sounds toward
the ears set on either side of the
wide, flat face. The incoming
sounds allow the owl to pinpoint
the direction of the prey.

   The ears of many owls are
slightly or strongly asymmetrical,
meaning that the right ear is
located somewhat higher on
the skull than the left ear. This
enables them to judge both hor-
izontal and vertical distance to
their prey. The ears of Great
Horned Owls are symmetrical
or nearly symmetrical, however,
indicating that they rely more
on sight than sound for identi-
fying, targeting, and tracking
prey. This is in keeping with
their role as a crepuscular as
well as nocturnal hunter.

Once the prey has been located, the Great Horned Owl launches into a short, powerful flight directly toward it. When flying toward its prey, the owl holds its head forward of the body to detect any prey movements and make minor adjustments in the flight path. Once within striking range, the owl extends its feet forward and opens its talons in a wide oval to snare the prey. The talon spread of a Great Horned Owl forms an oval nearly 4 to 8 inches (101.6 to 203.2 millimeters) in diameter, which is generally considerably larger than the targeted mouse or bird.

The additional talon spread provides an added measure of hunting success. Most prey are probably killed by the shock of the contact and the powerful, slashing talons, which close with a force measured at 28.7 pounds (13 kilograms), far more than adequate to sever the spinal column or crush the skull of its victim. If an animal is not immediately killed by the force of the impact, the owl clutches it securely, repeatedly squeezes and slashes the prey with its talons, and then dispatches it with one or more bites to the back of the head and neck.

The owl swallows small prey whole, usually headfirst, although sometimes it first strongly bites and crushes the skull. With larger prey, the owl dismembers it, strips meat from the bones with the powerful bill, and swallows it. Small bones may be swallowed whole, but larger bones are first crushed and then swallowed. If food is plentiful, the owl often decapitates its prey and eats only the brain, discarding the rest. Otherwise it may remove the feet and consume almost everything else.

Though Great Horned Owls are best equipped to hunt during the night, a hungry owl may hunt at any time. Although long considered a nocturnal predator, the Great Horned Owl often hunts in the twilight hours of dawn and dusk, when light conditions are uncertain and the advantage often lies with the hunter. Animals that are active at this time are said to have a crepuscular activity pattern, as opposed to a nocturnal or diurnal (daytime) activity pattern. If young are in the nest or food is in short supply, the owls may even extend their hunting activity into daylight hours, especially in the early morning or late afternoon. In the Great Basin Desert of central Utah, I often observed the late-afternoon hunting activity of Great Horned Owls on dark winter days with overcast skies.

The Great Horned Owl ranks among the most versatile of nocturnal hunters, able to hunt a wide variety of prey in many different kinds of habitats. Its nocturnal hunting abilities are best suited for relatively open habitats, such as open woodlands, orchards, groves, along woodland edges, over grasslands, desert scrub, wetlands, and along river courses. It readily hunts over open water and along shores of ponds and lakes for waterfowl and other waterbirds, including shorebirds, egrets, and herons.

Human-modified habitats may also provide good hunting grounds for this adaptive owl; clear-cuts or clear-cut swaths in and through woodlands, power lines, along roadways, canals, agricultural crop fields, maintained meadows, even large expanses of lawns such as found around airports and golf courses may be profitably hunted. Of all the large birds of prey, the Great Horned Owl probably benefits most from the fragmentation of eastern forests, as the resulting mix of tree-edged meadows and swaths provides both good perching sites and good open hunting habitat. As a hunter, the Great Horned Owl is probably somewhat less effective within deep woodlands and over thick brush, although its shorter and broader wings provide a margin of maneuverability that probably enables some hunting.

The Great Horned Owl relies mostly on the perch-and-wait method of hunting, usually sitting quietly on a perch and searching the immediate area with eyes and ears for suitable prey. When it sights prey, the owl makes short flights of about 100 yards (91.4 meters) or less, directly to the prey. In most areas, almost any elevated site that provides an overview of the immediate area may be used as a hunting perch—large branch of a live tree or dead snag, ledge, cliff line, rock outcrop, knoll, bridge, pier, abutment, fence post, or roof line of a barn or other outbuilding. Favorite perch sites in wooded areas are at or near the edges of clearings or more open parts of the woodland. In areas of low relief, silos, hay piles, or livestock watering troughs may serve as suitable hunting perches.

Occasionally I have seen hunting Great Horned Owls employ quartering flights somewhat similar to Northern Harrier *(Circus cyaneus)* hunting methods, in which one or both members of a pair fly back and forth just a few meters over low desert sagebrush. If the prey is missed on the first strike, these owls may alight and walk around the base of a bush or along a culvert or roadway ditch, apparently in search of the prey.

One evening under very windy conditions, I observed a Great Horned Owl hovering a few meters just above a grassy area like a kiting Red-tailed Hawk *(Buteo jamaicensis)* or hovering American Kestrel *(Falco sparverius)*. Hovering is an unusual hunting method for these big owls. While hovering, the owl faced into the wind, holding its position by strength of the wind and an occasional wingbeat. If the wind speed decreased, the owl beat its wings more frequently to maintain its position in the airstream. At intervals, the owl dipped and stooped toward prey, then returned to hovering. Strikes toward prey were very steep, almost vertical stoops into the tall grass, with the owl plummeting down on the prey. If the owl missed the prey, it either abandoned the hunt and flew to another, nearby spot or returned to hovering and resumed searching the same immediate area.

Great Horned Owls may abandon their aerial domain to walk awkwardly about the ground, searching through brush, along woodland edge, around the base of trees, or in wetland shallows for prey. Stomach contents containing invertebrates such as beetles, grasshoppers, or scorpions probably reflect this hunting method. A Great Horned Owl found dead near Mammoth, Arizona, for example, contained the remains of five centipedes, one tarantula, one mantid, and one long-nosed snake.

The Great Horned Owl has also been observed hawking insects such as beetles or grasshoppers in flight. Hawking is a hunting method often seen in flycatchers, such as the Eastern Kingbird *(Tyrannus tyrannus)* or Eastern Phoebe *(Sayornis phoebe),* in which the bird sits quietly on a perch awaiting flights of aerial insects. The bird swoops down to snatch an insect, then returns to its perch to await another hawking opportunity.

Most information about how Great Horned Owls hunt has been obtained by watching an individual forage during the late-evening hours. One crisp early morning in February, I was able to watch a pair of owls hunting part of their sagebrush-covered territory. The two owls kept quartering back and forth around a small juniper. A closer look revealed a badly shaken jackrabbit huddled beneath the tree, partly hidden in the folds of the gnarled trunk. By turns, one or the other owl flew just above the juniper while the other flew a watchful distance away. I may have been witnessing their efforts at team hunting, but the event proved inconclusive, because they flew off as I approached too closely, hoping to observe the outcome.

The opportunism in food habits exhibited by Great Horned Owls is matched by few nocturnal or diurnal birds of prey. Their ability to employ different hunting methods for different types of prey and to readily switch from one to another depending on the microhabitat of available prey lends much to their hunting success and, therefore, to their ecological success. When this is coupled with their ability to draw from a diverse variety of animals for food, the portrait of an extremely efficient hunter emerges.

Given its broad geographic range spanning the better part of two continents, the Great Horned Owl probably takes a greater variety of prey than any other owl, and most species of diurnal birds of prey as well. In fact, when driven by hunger, it has been known to take almost any animal—from worms and grasshoppers weighing a fraction of a gram to medium-sized birds and mammals weighing several thousand grams.

This owl's diet includes an extraordinarily wide variety of animals: mammals, birds, amphibians, reptiles, fish, and invertebrates. Throughout much of its range, at least in North America, the Great Horned Owl takes a consistently higher percentage of mammals than any other group, often 90 percent or more of its diet in terms of biomass. Though this may include any of the small to medium-size mammals that occur within its territory, this owl seems to rely most heavily on prey populations of rabbits and hares; where these are lacking or in low numbers, various populations of ground squirrels are staple components.

The list of mammals taken by Great Horned Owls includes virtually the entire spectrum of small American mammals: shrews, moles, mice, pocket mice, chipmunks, gophers, tree squirrels, flying squirrels, rats, kangaroo rats, weasels, bats, muskrats, minks, wood rats, raccoons, prairie dogs, marmots, skunks, porcupines, and an occasional house cat. In Latin America, mammalian prey includes viscacha, rabbits, and various marsupial species. Chuck LaRue, the noted Arizona birder and avid naturalist, witnessed a Great Horned Owl attack and kill a bobcat, which probably approaches the upper size limit of prey that this powerful owl can handle. Great Horned Owls seem to ignore the usually effective defenses of porcupines and skunks. Owls that prey on porcupines frequently carry their embedded quills for some time, although they seem to survive well enough. Though most predators avoid skunks, the Great Horned Owl is not deterred by the strong scent of its spray. Some Great Horned Owl pairs bring so many skunks to their young that their nest can be located by the odor alone. The smell of skunk may linger for years.

The diet of mammals is most frequently supplemented by birds, which at certain times of year may even become the Great Horned Owl's preferred prey, especially during the nesting and migratory seasons, when birds are more plentiful or more vulnerable. Birds taken as prey include ducks both wild and tame, shorebirds, gulls, egrets, bitterns, coots, loons, woodcocks, grouse, doves, pigeons, woodpeckers, and innumerable species of songbirds. Some of the larger waterfowl prey recorded are the Mallard, Canada Goose, Western Grebe, and Great Blue Heron. Ducks and other waterbirds are frequently taken during migration, and this owl is especially adept at snaring sleeping waterfowl as they rest on the surface of lakes and ponds.

The Great Horned Owl is also a noted predator of nesting birds and their nestlings. For songbirds, in addition to the nestling stage, the time just after fledging is their most vulnerable period, as they are learning how to fly, find shelter, and avoid enemies. Great Horned Owls are adroit at picking off inexperienced fledglings of thrushes, wrens, cardinals, and a host of other songbirds, which may constitute nearly half their diet during the late spring and early summer.

Ground-dwelling birds such as pheasants, quail, and grouse can be important food items, and Great Horned Owls are especially well known for their depredations on crows, starlings, pigeons, and other species that communally roost in large numbers. They are also noted for plucking territorial males from their singing perches, particularly during the late-evening hours, when songbirds are busily proclaiming their territories. In fact, any birds that occupy relatively open roosting sites may be picked off in the late-evening hours.

Great Horned Owls also seem to view the other owls as likely food sources, preying upon them when the opportunity arises. Any owl within the home range of a Great Horned Owl is likely at risk: Barn Owls, Barred Owls, Spotted Owls, Long-eared and Short-eared Owls, Burrowing Owls, Eastern and Western Screech Owls, and Northern Saw-whet Owls have all been recorded as Great Horned Owl food. While I was censusing Eastern Screech Owls by playing tape-recorded screech owl song in southern Connecticut, Great Horned Owls sometimes responded by silently flying in and landing on an overhead branch nearby. During my routine monitoring of two radio-transmitted screech owls, I tracked them to previously known roost sites but was unable to locate the owls. After extensively searching the area, I eventually located the transmitters, still working but twisted, bent, and deeply embedded in Great Horned Owl pellets, testimony to the toughness of the bird's digestive tract.

Great Horned Owls similarly hold little respect for the diurnal raptors with which they sometimes share the landscape, considering them just another food source to be exploited as opportunity permits. They specialize in robbing raptor nests at night, when the advantage of surprise is with this powerful owl. Adults at the nest and nestlings are frequent victims. The long list of diurnal raptors that are taken as prey include Red-tailed, Red-shouldered, Ferruginous, Broad-winged, and Swainson's Hawks; Osprey; Northern Goshawk; Cooper's and Sharp-shinned Hawks; Prairie and Peregrine Falcons; and American Kestrel. The size, strength, and agility of hawks make them more difficult targets during daylight hours, although the great horned is especially adroit at capturing recently fledged, and therefore inexperienced, young of raptors such as peregrines, much to the displeasure of the Peregrine Fund scientists.

Other foods I have found in Great Horned Owl pellets during years with low jackrabbit populations include scorpions, grasshoppers, lizards, and snakes. The last can apparently pose a problem, as several naturalists have reported instances of Great Horned Owls tangling unsuccessfully with large black snakes. In habitats where vertebrates are lacking or in short supply, the Great Horned Owl diet may incorporate a much greater percentage and variety of invertebrate prey, such as worms, crickets, centipedes, and ground beetles. In wetland and waterway habitats, prey may include crayfish, hellgrammites, frogs, toads, salamanders, and many species of fish, among them suckers, chubs, perch, bluegills, sunfish, catfish, and bullheads. Whether these are taken as carrion washed up on the lakeshore or caught while wading in shallows has never been determined.

Like many other birds of prey, Great Horned Owls may store remains of prey not consumed and even occasionally kill more prey than they can eat and store them in stockpiles called caches. They are especially noted for stockpiling food at their nests. In good jackrabbit years in central Utah, I have found nests containing the remains of as many as eleven jackrabbits, spilling out over the nest rim and crowding the already cramped quarters of the young owls. That indefatigable compiler of bird facts, Arthur Cleveland Bent, related many descriptions of Great Horned Owl nests with huge stockpiles of prey: One nest found by Major Bendire contained remains of a mouse, muskrat, rabbit, eleven rats, two eels, four bullheads, four ruffed grouse, and one woodcock, the whole weighing 18 pounds. Another nest contained the remains of black ducks, rabbits, rats, snakes, phalarope, rail, woodcock, bobwhite, flicker, pheasant, and several smaller birds.

Winter food caches are tapped as needed and may be crucial to the owl's survival during extended periods of deep snow or low prey availability. Northern owls are especially noted for their rather unusual behavior of defrosting frozen prey by sitting on it until the meat has thawed sufficiently to be eaten.

As with all owls, Great Horned Owl prey is digested to a liquid consistency in a stomach characterized by high acidity and proteolytic activity, and then passed into the intestinal tract. The undigested remains of prey—mostly fur, feathers, bones, and teeth, along with indigestible organic matter such as seeds and the chitinous shells of invertebrates—are compacted over several hours into a small ball called a pellet. The process of digestion takes only a few hours, but pellet formation may not be completed for several more hours, depending on the meal. The pellet is eventually regurgitated in a reflexive choking motion that casts the pellet out of the mouth. As the process of pellet formation takes several hours, the pellets that are cast actually represent the remains of the previous day's food. When food is scarce, the bird may not cast a pellet for several days, but if food is abundant and meals are frequent, it casts pellets more often.

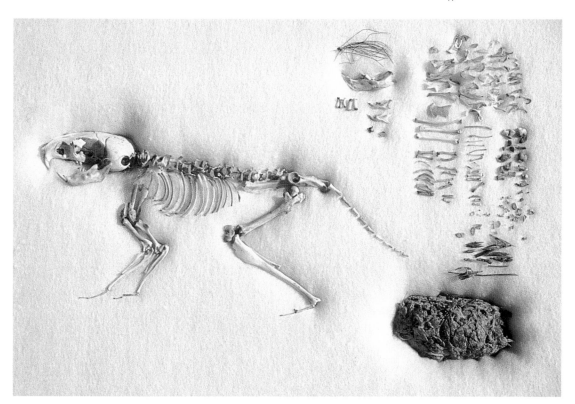

Because pellets contain the remains of prey, their analysis can reveal much about the Great Horned Owl's daily and seasonal food habits. Owl biologists collect pellets from beneath known owl roost sites and carefully dissect them, separating skulls, mandibles, other bones, feathers, fur, and other identifiable materials. The skeleton shown on the left was reconstructed from bones found in the pellet. The bones are then compared with museum specimens to identify prey species. For the great horned and many other owl species, this is an important form of research, because it permits a reasonable determination of their food habits with little or no disturbance of the birds.

Courtship and Nesting

3

No other temperate bird of prey nests as early as the Great Horned Owl. In Florida, along the Gulf Coast, in Southern California, and throughout much of the Southwest, Great Horned Owl nests containing eggs have been recorded in November and December, although January is the most common nesting month here. In the central and northern tier of states, nesting is initiated a month or two later, generally anywhere from mid-February into March. Even in the most northern parts of its range, the Great Horned Owl is still one of the first species to nest: In Alaska, northern Canada, and Labrador, it may complete its clutch of eggs before the end of April. Nesting is much earlier across much of Latin America, where fresh eggs may be recorded in late September or October, and young owls are found in the nest in late November and December.

Throughout the snowier parts of the Great Horned Owl's range, it is not unusual to spot a female half buried in fresh snow, resolutely incubating her new clutch of eggs. Any disturbance during this time may have critical consequences; the eggs cannot be left unattended in freezing temperatures for more than a few minutes, as they quickly freeze. The presence of addled eggs (eggs in which the embryo has failed to develop) in nests may indicate undue disturbance early in the nesting season. Sometimes the female will lay a second clutch of eggs and incubate them—often successfully—among the addled eggs.

The exact timing of the nesting season frequently varies from year to year, depending mostly on the severity of winter temperatures and the availability of food. The nesting season may begin a month or so earlier following a mild winter, but it may be delayed for several weeks after an unusually severe winter with extended periods of freezing temperatures and snow cover. Over a five-year period, I noted dramatic differences in the timing of nesting among a Great Horned Owl population in the eastern Great Basin Desert of Utah. They completed clutches several weeks earlier after warmer winters, but colder and snowier winters delayed the onset of nesting by several weeks. The abundance or lack of prey may also influence the timing of nesting, or whether the birds even nest at all. In years of exceptional prey abundance, nesting may be initiated somewhat earlier than in years in which prey populations are low. In years of very low prey populations, fewer pairs of Great Horned Owls initiate nesting.

The start of the breeding season is signaled by courtship activities initiated by the male. Unmated males must first find a vacant territory to claim. They then both advertise their possession of the territory and call for a mate by vigorous singing bouts. These singing activities can begin in late fall and continue through winter months, but more commonly begin very early in the nesting season, late winter in most areas.

When singing, the male Great Horned Owl bows forward while simultaneously drooping his wings downward and cocking the tail upward. At each song, he puffs out his chest, displaying his white bib, which may help signal his location to a potential mate.

Territorial singing displays typically begin at dusk and continue for an hour or more into darkness. Another major bout of territorial singing may occur in the late hours of night, just before dawn. Occasionally I have heard males begin singing bouts an hour or so before darkness and extend them into daylight, especially in late winter. If a potential mate fails to respond, the territory-holding male may continue to sing until well into the breeding season.

To advertise territory and call for mates, Great Horned Owls use a three- to seven-note song consisting of a low, deep *whoo-hoo, woo whoo-hoo* or *whoo, hoo-hoo-hoo, whooo, whooo*, with all of the syllables falling on the same note. Many variants of this song exist, one of which has been described as *guacouroutou-tou.* The owl's voice carries well and far in quiet woodlands and other habitats this owl claims. It has been likened to a faraway foghorn, a nocturnal dove, or a bass-voiced dog barking in the distance. Less frequently, a Great Horned Owl may utter a loud, piercing shriek or scream, but whether this signals a territorial dispute or proclamation is unknown.

Interested females respond to a male's advertisement by flying in and alighting near him. The male then switches from singing to courting in earnest. His courtship takes several forms, which may all be blended into a continuous event from start to finish. At first the excited male hops back and forth from branch to branch, always within sight of the female. He may call repeatedly during this performance, vigorously clack his bill, spread and flap his wings, or ruffle his feathers.

Sometimes the male interrupts these performances with courtship flights, in which he circles around the female, who generally sits, sometimes quietly watching but at other times taking no apparent notice. These flights may combine elements of aerial diving and swooping about, but the male soon returns and alights near the female. If she is receptive, he bashfully approaches her with great timidity or hesitancy. Any ruffling of feathers or apparent uninterest on the part of the female is met with renewed calling, hopping about from branch to branch, a vigorous clacking of the bill, or taking off on short flights.

As the female becomes increasingly receptive, the male approaches ever nearer. He initiates mutual preening and bill rubbing, to which she typically responds in like fashion. Sometimes the male approaches the

female with a food offering to show his hunting prowess. The pair-bond may be cemented by mutual flights in which both male and female fly off together, either side by side or with the male leading and the female following.

At the completion of courtship and pair formation, the two birds are united in their efforts to proclaim and defend the breeding territory and raise their brood. The pair will remain together throughout the year, maintaining the pair-bond through various behaviors, the most common of which is calling or duetting by both birds. Duets consist of alternate but synchronized calling back and forth between the male and female. They are generally begun by the female and may be conducted at any time of year but are most commonly observed very early in the owl breeding season, from late December through March.

In Connecticut woodlands, I have consistently heard pairs engage in duets lasting an hour or more. These begin in late September and continue through the fall months, usually at irregular periods. The duet patterns are similar to descriptions provided by Paul Johnsgard. In sequence, each member of a pair calls the territorial advertisement song. Each call lasts about three to four seconds. Calls are separated by intervals of varying lengths but generally about ten to fifty seconds. The male calls with a deeper voice, the female with a higher-pitched voice.

As the duet progresses, the pair seems to become increasingly excited and the male responds more quickly, often before the female has completed her call. After an hour or so, the synchronized calls gradually decline in frequency until duetting ceases. Duets by pairs are thought to help maintain and strengthen the pair-bond.

Great Horned Owl pairs may stay together for many years. They may roost together or near one another. If they roost at different sites, the male generally begins the evening activities by flying to the female's roost and calling softly to her. Then they depart together to begin the night's activities.

Great Horned Owl pairs vigorously proclaim and defend their territory. Either one or both members of a pair participate in territorial advertisement, either by individual singing bouts—more often conducted by the male than the female—or by duetting. In New England woodlands, I have sometimes heard three or four pairs calling back and forth, each advertising its own territory. Generally these advertising exhibitions are initiated by one pair proclaiming its territory, and the singing activity is taken up by neighboring pairs.

Males more frequently respond aggressively to the presence of an intruding owl, but sometimes both members of a pair react. Owls defending their territory usually respond by flying toward and around the intruder, sometimes stooping toward it, loudly calling or vigorously clacking the bill throughout the encounter. The male may grapple with intruders that don't immediately depart. Following the encounter, one or both members of a pair escort the intruder out of the territory. Combat to the death such as seen on page 46 is probably uncommon.

A Great Horned Owl population is normally nearly sedentary, remaining in the same area for years. Southward incursions of northern owls occur when their prey populations precipitously decline, and there is some evidence of montane-dwelling Great Horned Owls moving from higher to lower elevations in winter and returning to the higher elevations the following spring. Otherwise, adults are entirely sedentary, often retaining and remaining within the same territory for many years. For much of the year, a Great Horned Owl occupies its home range, an undefended or only weakly defended area claimed by a pair or an individual owl. Home ranges of adjacent owls may overlap extensively, and limited intrusions are occasionally tolerated.

At the beginning of the breeding season, a pair establishes or reestablishes its nesting territory, a portion of the home range that it defends. This is generally smaller than the home

range, from several hundred to several thousand acres in size. Territory shape is a function of topography. Territories of riverine habitats are often elongated along the course of the stream, extending outward along its length. Most of the Great Horned Owl territories that I mapped in the Great Basin canyons encompassed much of the canyon and extended fan-shaped out into the surrounding valleys. By the start of the breeding season, the landscape is subdivided into a mosaic of Great Horned Owl nesting territories.

The territories are proclaimed nightly at favorite singing perches, which are almost always elevated sites that provide a commanding view of at least part of the territory. Pairs have several perch sites for proclaiming territories, some or all of which might be used in a single night.

In addition to territorial pairs, Great Horned Owl populations also include nonterritorial individuals, called floaters. Most of those birds remain unmated during the breeding season, but some may form temporary pairings. Every breeding population of Great Horned Owls may include sizable numbers of floaters, which are unmated first-year birds but sometimes older birds as well.

Because they are at the periphery of nesting events, the shadowy role of floaters is poorly known and, prior to the advent of radiotelemetry, difficult to study. Floaters typically occupy and hang about the periphery of established territories and may occasionally temporarily intrude during hunting forays. Regular and prolonged intrusions are aggressively met by the territorial pair until the floater is prompted to leave, usually under escort by one or both members of the territorial pair. Although an important component of the population, floaters typically occupy suboptimum habitats, and thus any decrease in food supply will affect them long before territorial pairs. Floaters play an important role as a readily available source of mate birds should one member of a mated pair be killed. Exactly how floaters learn about a death is unknown, but the replacement of a lost mate often takes place within just a few days.

Like most other owls, great horned do not construct their own nests, but appropriate nests of other species. If these are lacking or unsuitable, they choose almost any sheltered site in which to lay their eggs and raise their young. Among raptors, Great Horned Owls are undoubtedly the most versatile in nest site selection. Because they are among the earliest-nesting birds, they can advantageously appropriate nests of a wide variety of avian species. The Great Horned Owl will use the nest of almost any sizable hawk, including Red-tailed Hawks, Broad-wing Hawks, Cooper's Hawks, and Northern Goshawks, along with Golden or Bald Eagles or Osprey. Great Blue Heron nests provide ample room for an owl and her brood. If nests of these larger birds are lacking, this owl may appropriate nests of ravens or crows. I have also found them occupying the broad, flat tops of Monk Parakeet nests in Connecticut and the flattened nests of magpies in Utah and Nevada.

Great Horned Owls occasionally use the compacted leafy nests of squirrels, large tree hollows, the tops of snags, grape tangles, or even debris-filled crotches of trees. Their use of tree hollows and snags increases in old-growth woodlands, where these sites may be fairly common. A female sitting on her eggs will be mostly hidden as she hunkers down on the nest. Her cryptic coloration also helps conceal her at the nest site.

In the mountains and canyons of the West and other treeless regions, Great Horned Owls usually nest in cliff lines, ledges, crevices, or small caves, especially if they contain the nest remains of other species, hawks, falcons, or ravens. Crevices and shallow caves seem to be favorites and may be used even if not used previously by other species, the female owl simply scooping and lining a shallow scrape with a few feathers and laying her eggs directly on the dirt or barely covered rock. In the cacti deserts of the Southwest, favored sites include hawk nests in giant saguaro. In some areas, the owls may nest directly on the ground in the shadow of a bush, or less commonly, in the abandoned entrance of an old badger, coyote, or kit fox den.

If suitable natural sites are lacking, Great Horned Owls will readily nest in human-modified landscapes. Nests have been found in niches, crevices, and caves in abandoned rock quarries and sometimes even at the edge of an active quarry. Great Horned Owls have also been known to nest on towers, old barns, and other abandoned structures, bridges, piers, poles, power lines, and haystacks.

Stick nests are normally used for only one breeding season, as Great Horned Owls don't refurbish nests, and they generally fall into such disrepair by the end of the nesting season that they can't be used the following year. Ledges, caves, and other permanent sites may be used for many years, sometimes in succession and sometimes once every few years. Whether this represents the genetic continuity of a pair and their offspring or is simply the reflection of an optimum nest site is unknown. Some of the Great Horned Owl nest sites that I found in central Utah in 1966 are still in use today, although none was occupied for more than two to three years in succession. Reoccupancy rates have been consistently higher for nest sites located in crevices and cliff niches, lower for sites in caves and on sheltered ledges.

The male may choose several nest sites and offer them to the female, who makes the actual selection. The male walks around and about a potential nest site, often trampling and scratching the substrate, all the while calling and uttering a variety of mostly guttural noises. The female watches his performance and then makes her selection. After she has chosen a nest site, she may modify it slightly or not at all. Depending on materials available, she may at least rearrange the sticks, bark, twigs, and other debris in the nest. Some females do very little rearranging, merely scooping or scraping away a shallow hole, which she then lines with her breast feathers or bits of fur and feathers of prey.

Once she has prepared the nest, she lays her eggs. Great Horned Owl eggs are large, nearly spherical in shape, coarse in texture, and dull to slightly glossy white in color. They are about 2.1 to 2.2 inches (53 to 56 centimeters) in length, 1.8 to 1.9 inches (45 to 47 millimeters) wide, and weigh 1.7 to 1.9 ounces (48 to 54 grams). Egg sizes differ slightly among subspecies. The first eggs of a clutch are generally larger, and there is often a progressive decrease in size from the first to the last egg of a clutch.

The number of eggs laid in a completed clutch is called the clutch size. The average Great Horned Owl clutch size varies with latitude, weather, and food supply, generally two or three eggs, rarely one, four, or more eggs. Clutches of five or six eggs have been reported, but these are quite rare. The eggs of a clutch are normally laid at two-day intervals, although intervals up to seven days have been reported. Clutches that are lost or destroyed may be replaced if it is early in the nesting season.

Clutches are typically somewhat larger in wetter years than in drier years, presumably because wetter years increase basic productivity of terrestrial ecosystems, which increases prey abundance. There appears to be a correlation between the number of eggs in a clutch and the local food supply. Clutch sizes in good prey years are often considerably larger than in poor prey years. For example, in a central Utah study, clutch sizes averaged 3.3 eggs in years of high jackrabbit abundance, but decreased to an average of 2.0 eggs per clutch when jackrabbit populations declined. During periods of exceptionally low food availability, Great Horned Owls may choose a nest but not lay a clutch, or may abandon the nest before the clutch is completed.

Upon laying the first egg, the female immediately begins incubation. The female of the pair does most of the sitting on the eggs, although the male takes her place at certain times, especially in the late evening, shortly after sunset but before full darkness, when he sits over the eggs while she flies off to hunt.

The ritual attending the male's nightly relief of the female was described by Frederick Baumgartner, who watched the ceremony from a nearby blind. At first the male hooted from a distance, then he flew in and alighted near the nest site. At the nest, the male uttered a soft *quawk, quawk, waugth! hoo-hoo! quawk, quawk, quawk, quawk.* Both birds nodded and bowed to one another, then engaged in mutual bill rubbing. After a short time, the female stood up, bowed, and stepped out of the nest as the male stepped carefully in, arranged the eggs with his bill, and settled over them.

The male's exact role in incubation duties is unknown. The female develops an incubation patch, but the male does not develop such a patch, suggesting a limited involvement in incubating the eggs. In central Utah, I occasionally found both members of a pair sitting side by side in the nest, although I could not determine whether the male was actually helping incubate the eggs or merely keeping his female company.

The incubation period for Great Horned Owls is thirty to thirty-seven days, with an average of thirty-three days. Throughout the incubation period, the female remains almost constantly at the nest and on the eggs, especially during the short days and long, cold nights. She dozes during much of the day, occasionally opening one or both eyes partially to alertly scan the immediate landscape. During the night, the female is awake and alert and continues to incubate the eggs. She occasionally stands, stretches, checks the eggs, then settles down on them again.

While the female sits on the eggs, the male supplies her with food during the night and patiently maintains a vigil about the nest site as he dozes away the day. He roosts in a secluded spot generally within 100 yards (91.4 meters) of the nest site, from which he can keep an eye on everything. If the nest is approached, it is generally the male who first notices the intruder, alerting the female by a long *hoot.* Unfortunately, this is often the limit of his defense of the nest and female, as he rarely leaves the security of his secluded perch, even when intruders approach the nest.

On the other hand, the female closely and jealously guards her eggs. If an intruder appears, she hunkers down as much as possible, with only her eyes and ear tufts appearing above the rim of the nest. Females are most reluctant to leave their eggs, departing at almost the last minute in the face of humans or other large intruders. She typically flies only a short distance away, where she keeps a close eye on activities at the nest. Nest robbers such as ravens and magpies in the West or opossums and raccoons in the East are rarely given the opportunity to steal eggs of Great Horned Owls.

4

Growth and Development of the Young

As hatching time nears, the young can sometimes be heard peeping and moving about within the eggs. Hatching occurs asynchronously at about two-day intervals, and the eggs of a clutch usually hatch in the order that they were laid. Therefore, in clutches of three or four eggs, the oldest young may be nearly a week older than the youngest. The uneven-aged young in the nest is an ecological hedge; if the food supply decreases and the adults are unable to provide sufficient food to feed all the young, the oldest survive at the expense of the youngest. In extreme cases, the youngest member of the nest becomes progressively weaker from starvation and may die or be killed and eaten by its older siblings.

Hatching success of Great Horned Owl clutches is typically a function of several factors, including the amount of disturbance at or near the nest site during the incubation period, weather conditions, and the availability of food. In every nesting population, a certain percentage of eggs fail to hatch. Some unhatched eggs are infertile, and others may have been frozen when left unattended and become addled.

Probably because of the attention of the female to her eggs, the number of unhatched eggs in Great Horned Owl nests is typically low. In a long-term study of Great Horned Owl nesting success conducted near Cincinnati, only 97 of 1,667 eggs failed to hatch, for a success rate of 94.2 percent. The fact that 76 of the unhatched eggs were in nests that contained no young suggests that either an unusually high degree of disturbance occurred at those nest sites during incubation or the females were inexperienced, or possibly both. The availability of food may also have been a factor. Studies by myself and Canadian owl researcher C. Stuart Houston have shown that the percentage of unhatched eggs is higher in years of low prey abundance, probably because the owls must spend so much time hunting for food that they are unable to devote sufficient time to incubating the eggs. Unless removed by predators, unhatched eggs remain in the nest until trampled by the adults or developing young.

When first hatched, young birds of prey are entirely helpless. Their immediate survival is entirely dependent on the adults, which brood, care for, feed, and protect them. Young Great Horned Owls are brooded entirely by the female, who maintains an almost continual vigil at the nest until they are about two weeks old. Depending on the ambient temperature, she carefully settles over them to brood. In the cold of winter, she constantly broods the young. If temperatures become too warm, she shades them with her wings or by placing her body between them and the light source. If she leaves the nest to feed or for nest sanitation, she carefully gathers them together on her return, uttering soft *hut, hut, hut* cries, to which the young respond with even softer whimpers.

During the first weeks, the female also maintains sole responsibility for feeding the young, while the male typically confines his role to delivering food to the nest. To feed the young, the female tears the food into small pieces, which she carefully and tenderly places into their open bills. The male's delivery rate of prey depends on three things: the number of young in the nest that need to be fed (along with the female, who often depends on her mate for food at this time), the availability of prey, and the size of individual prey. A single large prey such as a ground squirrel or duck might suffice for a night, especially if delivered soon after dark, or the male may make several trips to the nest, carrying small rodents or large invertebrates with each trip.

If the food supply is low or the male fails to deliver sufficient food, the female may leave the nest and hunt for food for herself and her nestlings. The timely delivery of food to the nest is especially critical during this period, and the loss of a mate threatens the survival of the young and may often result in the failure of the nest. Rarely do single parents successfully raise a brood of young owls, although I did observe a single parent, probably the female, successfully raise a brood of one during a good jackrabbit year after her mate had been struck and killed on a nearby highway.

The care and sanitation of the nest also are the responsibility of the female. As in many other birds, female Great Horned Owls may eat the exudates of the young until they are old enough to defecate over the edge of the nest, which begins at about the fourth week. There are a few reports of adults moving nestlings from the nest site to another location, usually within 100 yards (91.4 meters). These events may follow the destruction of a nest or perhaps result from frequent disturbance at the nest site.

Newly hatched Great Horned Owls resemble miniature balls of fluff and weigh about half a pound (35 to 50 grams). The young are covered with grayish white or dirty gray down and have ungainly legs and pink feet. The soft down provides excellent insulation for the young. Remnants of the egg tooth on the upper bill and the dried yolk sac are retained for several days, sometimes more.

The altricial young are blind and weak, unable to stand or to feed themselves. Their eyes may partially open within a few days but generally do not fully open before the ninth or tenth day. The young already possess the protective nictitating membranes, sometimes called the third eyelids, which function to keep the eyes moist and protected. This membrane will develop more clearly as they become older. The young very quickly show instinctive responses and reflexes related to feeding, brooding, and fears.

Within a few hours of hatching, the young are able to react to noises, movements, and pressures about the nest that signal the arrival of the adult. They reflexively respond to an adult by crawling or rocking in the direction of the adult with their mouths gaped open. If a bit of food is placed in the mouth, their swallowing is reflexive. Unable to stand, they clench their feet in a tripod stance and rock back and forth toward the noise, all the while emitting a raspy feeding chirp to attract attention. Young that are not fed collapse back into the nest, remaining immobile until they gather up enough strength to try again.

Other behaviors related to brooding and fear also soon manifest. The young remain quietly under the protective feathers of the female or, less frequently, the male during brooding. If uncovered, they attempt to crawl back and farther under the adult by pushing along with their legs. Young unable to find an adult huddle together or emit a whimpering chirp much lower and longer than the rasping chirp they give when hungry.

At this age, fear behavior occurs in response to loud noises or rocking movements of the nest or of the limbs in which the nest is constructed. Fearful young shut their eyes and play possum, crouch, or passively cower together in the center of the nest. As they get older, the young become more attentive and alert to any movements near the nest that may pose a threat to them. Nearly mature young switch tactics and respond aggressively to intruders by vigorously clapping their bills, fluffing their feathers, and arching up their wings to make themselves appear larger and more formidable.

Young that are older still will attack and attempt to drive intruders away by determinedly striking out with open talons. Very large intruders, however, may drive the young off the nest as they try to escape. This last is particularly worrisome to owl biologists who climb into a nest to band the young, as the birds' awkward flight and inexperienced landing attempts may result in injury.

After her eggs have hatched and there are young in the nest, the female is bolder, more assertive, difficult to approach, and dangerous when provoked. She is very reluctant to leave recently hatched young in the nest, especially during periods of cold or freezing temperatures. She hunkers down on the nest, closely brooding the young, spreading her wings to protectively cover and conceal them, a behavior called mantling, also used to cover freshly killed prey. She does not leave until the intruder is within a few meters.

When flushed, she usually flies only a few meters away before landing. Both she and her mate may respond to intruders by hooting, head bobbing, and a loud, resonant bill clicking. Occasionally a desperate female may resort to fluttering about the ground like a grouse with a broken wing, a common ruse used by many species of birds but rarely seen in owls. The female normally returns to the nest within a few minutes after the intruders have left and appears to check the safety of the young closely before settling down with them. As the young get older, the female becomes progressively more aggressive in her defense of the young. She also becomes increasingly reluctant to depart the nest, and if she does so, flies only a short distance away to protest the intrusion.

Through it all, the male member of the family seems to take only a mild-mannered interest in the events at the nest, almost to the point of being timid. While the female is vigorously attacking the intruder, the male can be heard off in the distance, softly, almost shyly, hooting his protests. Though I have been chased away or deterred from investigating nests too closely by female Great Horned Owls, I have never had a male pursue an attack with the same aggressiveness as the female, which, in Great Horned Owls, is always the stronger sex.

Within a couple weeks after they have hatched, the young owls grow stronger and more alert. They are now able to distinguish between random noises and movements and those related to feeding. They now spend a lot of their time standing about impatiently awaiting the arrival of an adult with food. An adult arriving at the nest is met by a rushing mob of juvenile owls, all begging insistently and persistently for food. At first their food consists of small bits of meat, hair, and bone torn from the prey and placed in the back of the gaping mouths of the young. The bone and hair fragments probably stimulate the development of digestive organs. At two to three weeks old, the young owl's grayish white down is now edged by brownish barring, but the facial disk has not yet developed.

Within three weeks, curiosity and play instinct are clearly evident. The young grow more and more curious about the minutiae of their nest, moving food remains about and occasionally picking them up and dropping them. They often seem to investigate their toes, staring at them for long periods of time and reaching down to peck them gently. Moving objects such as birds in flight, airplanes overhead, or passing cars may also attract their attention. By this time, the young are capable of peering closely at objects with those curious head motions characteristic of many owls. Sometimes, if a bird is really interested, the swaying turns into a circular motion, with head first moving clockwise, then in the reverse direction.

Pellet ejection by the young begins at this stage. Various species of birds expel pellets in different ways. Some perform violent contortions, then spit the pellet out. Other species, such as members of the crow family, cough up the pellet seemingly effortlessly, hold it in the bill, and drop it to the ground. The Great Horned Owl seems to be able to eject pellets effortlessly at any time of the day or night. Once a young owl releases a pellet, it often plays with it, picking it up, rolling it over in the nest, and examining it for edibility. When the bird finds it is not edible, it picks the pellet up with its foot and examines it further, until it finds an interest in something else and abandons the pellet.

By the third week, the young are able to feed themselves to some extent, at least the older young, although the female may continue to feed them for at least another week or two. The young birds may pick up small fragments of meat left about the nest in their bills and swallow them. They now swallow whole small prey brought to the nest, such as mice and songbirds, always headfirst. If the prey is still alive, younger owls seem confused, observing it cautiously, as they have not yet learned how to kill it; older and more aggressive young may strike out at small prey and kill it. I have also seen a young owl grasp and squeeze a struggling mouse until it died. The bird then ignored the mouse, although it had been eaten on my next visit to the nest.

Hungry young call to the parents with a single loud note that sounds like a combination of a hiss and a scream. Older young become still more demanding and consequently noisier and noisier. Toward the end of the nesting season, I have sometimes been able to locate undiscovered nest sites by listening to the nightly hunger screams of a nest full of young Great Horned Owls.

At three to four weeks old, the young owl's natal grayish white down is rapidly being replaced with brownish juvenile feathers, and the wing primaries are just beginning to emerge from their sheaths. The young are now growing rapidly, the facial disk is developing, and the "horns" are just beginning to grow. They are increasingly alert and react aggressively to intruders at the nest by vigorous bill clapping and hissing. By the fourth week, sometimes earlier, the young attempt nest sanitation by expelling their wastes over the edge of the nest.

At four to five weeks old, the young show the gradual transition of feather coloration, from downy white to grayish to the brownish mottling and barring of adult owls. The orangish facial disk, heavily edged in black, is increasingly well developed at this stage.

Toward the end of the fourth week, sometimes earlier, the young become increasingly alert and mobile about the nest. They stretch and test their wings, sometimes flapping them as they half jump and half flap from one place to another. The young owls also begin to change the position in which they sleep, no longer sleeping with their bills underneath their scapulars. Instead, they sleep standing up, with their heads hunched on their shoulders and all their feathers fluffed out.

For all birds, fledging time is fraught with difficulty and danger. The young birds must learn how to fly and to find food and shelter, while avoiding enemies and accidents. This is the most vulnerable period of their lives, and the survival rate of young owls is often less than 50 percent during this time. In order to ensure their success and survival, the young of most birds, including Great Horned Owls, typically spend time in company of the adults as they learn and perfect the basic survival skills.

For young Great Horned Owls, fledging takes place fairly quickly for all the young of a nest. Around the sixth week in the nest, the young become increasingly interested in flight. They spend a lot of time preparing their flight feathers by running them between the mandibles of their bills, carefully rearranging the ends. They are now able to climb by walking and flapping. If the nest is in a tree, fledging is often preceded by branching, in which the older young abandon the nest to climb about the nearby branches, returning to the nest when an adult arrives with food. At this time they are often active during both day and night, clambering among the branches and continuously begging food from the adults. The development of this climbing ability also proves useful among young birds that may have fallen out of the nest. Their commotion increases their exposure and vulnerability, and at this stage, the young are susceptible to a range of accidents, such as falling out of the tree or falling prey to a hawk or other bird of prey.

Sometime between the sixth and seventh weeks, the young learn how to fly. By this time, their weight gain, so rapid at first, has leveled off, and they are about three-quarters the size of an adult in weight. The feather sheaths have been mostly shed, and although they still have some gray around the head, the wings and body are nearly fully feathered like the adults, enabling better flight control.

Even different-aged young often take their first flights within a few days of one another. Like young of almost all other birds approaching their first flights, the young owls increasingly flex and flap their wings as they stand about the nest or on the nearby branches. As they become stronger, these flapping bouts increasingly become a helicopterlike hovering a few centimeters above the ground.

Soon thereafter, the young take their first flights, which consist mostly of launching off a branch or cliff face and awkwardly, very awkwardly at times, frantically flapping and flying and gliding to the nearest convenient landing site. First landings are often a comical and desperate controlled crash, as the young owls frantically grasp and desperately hang on to the nearest branch. They often end sprawled across a ledge or hanging upside down on a tree branch, or tumble down to the ground. In only a short time, often before the end of the first day out of the nest, the young owls become increasingly adept fliers, although landings may take longer to perfect. Within a few days, the young are flying about reasonably well, but they don't begin to approach the flight skills of the adults until they are about ten or twelve weeks old.

For the first few weeks after fledging, the young remain near the nest site, sometimes returning to the site or nearby each night. They spend most of their time loafing, exercising their wings, and most of all, begging the adults for food with special hunger calls that sound like a hawk's raspy scream.

The adults are kept quite busy hunting food for the young, and their appearance with food is met by a mob scene of sorts, as the young chase them about, persistently calling to be fed. During this time, the adults may occasionally leave a prey item for the young, often at the old nest site. The young are now left on their own, to tear the food apart and eat it. At this stage, the more aggressive young, or perhaps the more hungry, may even attempt to follow the adults about for food.

During this postfledging period, the adults maintain a cursory watch of the young throughout the day and night. They roost within sight or sound of the young, although rarely in the same tree or other site. To keep in contact with the young, the adults utter short barking notes: *whar, who, whar, oo-who-o-o-o-ooh.* They are always alert for any danger. At the first sign of an intruder, the adult owls signal their young to be quiet and remain still with a loud *wac-wac* call.

As in virtually all birds, this juvenile dependency period is a most critical time for the young to develop their hunting skills. They have to learn how to find prey, how to strike and kill it, and how to effectively dismember it for swallowing. Casual observations suggest that young Great Horned Owls learn partly by watching the adults and partly by experiments on their own. Pellet recoveries suggest that the young first try their skills on small and slow prey, such as grasshoppers, beetles, scorpions, and other such invertebrates, supplemented by small rodents, often newly independent mice and squirrels. Only gradually do they acquire the strength, dexterity, and skills necessary to successfully take larger prey. Inexperienced young appear to sometimes take on prey that is too large or too formidable and either miss capturing the prey entirely, as when they are chasing down squirrels, or attack and then abandon the prey when it is a larger animal, such as a woodchuck.

The young remain in company with the parents for most of the summer and often into the fall months. Many young owls remain in the immediate vicinity of their natal territory, and some occasionally venture back into it. Although returning young may even attempt food begging, they are quickly and determinedly driven back out by one or both adults.

Following their enforced removal from their natal territory, the young may keep company with one another for a brief time before wandering in search of an unoccupied territory to claim. This can be a difficult time for the young, because the best territories are generally already claimed. Most often, the young become part of the nonterritorial pool of birds called floaters which must await the availability of a suitable territory to claim. Most of the larger birds of prey typically don't mature for several years. This may be partly a matter of sexual maturity and partly a function of the availability of territories. A small percentage of female

Great Horned Owls breed in their first year, but these are probably the exceptions. For the Great Horned Owl population, average age at breeding is about two years old, provided a territory is available.

If the young owls can survive the hazards of their first year, they have a reasonably good chance of living for several more years. Their survival rate varies from year to year directly with weather conditions and food supply. In good prey years, three-quarters or more of the young will survive through their first winter, but in years of low prey populations, only one in four or less of the first-year Great Horned Owls will survive.

If they can survive their first year, then their chances will increase somewhat each following year, presumably because they have acquired the necessary skills for finding food and shelter and avoiding enemies. Their survival chances are increased still further if they are able to claim and hold a territory, which will help ensure an adequate food supply, especially in lean prey years.

Great Horned Owls are the longest-lived of all North American owls, though exactly how long they actually survive in the wild is unknown. The longevity record is twenty-eight years and seven months, but this owl was banded at an unknown age, so it lived somewhat longer. The two longest records for Great Horned Owls banded as nestlings are twenty-two years and two months and twenty-one years and four months.

5

Conservation Ecology

In the wild, Great Horned Owls have few natural enemies. A few birds may fall victim to accidents, and some incautious owls occasionally become meals of other predators, such as eagles, bobcats, or lions, but these types of mortality are probably relatively rare. Most of the annual mortality of Great Horned Owls occurs during or shortly after the breeding season. Ravens, raccoons, opossums, and other nest robbers may steal an occasional egg or small young from a nest, but the most risky period is the time just after fledging, when the inexperienced young begin learning to fly and hunt while trying to avoid enemies. It is during this time that many of them fall victim to all sorts of accidents, some with fatal consequences: misjudged landings, flights into thick brush while pursuing prey, foraging opportunistically on road-killed animals, or tackling prey such as snakes, herons, egrets, bobcats, or wolverines which are either too large to be handled by an inexperienced hunter or simply too formidable.

Once the juvenile period is past, the Great Horned Owl has little to fear from other animals in its natural environment.

Ecologically, this owl has but three simple needs: a daytime roosting site, a suitable nest site, and an adequate food supply for itself and its young. Great Horned Owls are able to use a wide variety of roosting and nesting sites, and they are able to exploit almost any available prey base. Given their incredible flexibility and adaptability, these owls can survive in almost any American landscape if left undisturbed. But unfortunately, their coexistence with humans and within human-modified landscapes has often had a negative impact on Great Horned Owl populations, a trend that continues to this day.

The association between Great Horned Owls and humans has been long and often dismal. The ferocity and appetite of this remarkable owl, more than any other, aroused the ire of farmers, gamekeepers, and sportsmen. Long accustomed to viewing raptors with superstition and distrust, they variously described the Great Horned Owl as savage and sanguine, huge and unsociable, cannibalistic and morose, and the nemesis of the night. And probably more than any other predator, the Great Horned Owl lived up to its savage reputation. It proved the bane of farmers by snatching chickens, turkeys, and other barnyard animals with apparent ease. Great Horned Owls sometimes decimated entire chicken coops, often killing the birds and eating only their brains. Gamekeepers and sportsmen also fervently disliked it for its appetite for grouse, quail, duck, and wild turkey.

Gamekeepers, pigeon fanciers, sportsmen, and conservationists determined to protect wild birds were all united in their efforts to destroy the Great Horned Owl by shooting and trapping them whenever possible. So terrible was its reputation that the Great Horned Owl continued to be legally shot and trapped long after enlightened conservationists called loudly, persistently, and successfully for the protection of hawks, eagles, and most of the other species of owls.

To protect the domestic poultry of farmers and wild game for hunters, most states and Canadian provinces placed a bounty on Great Horned Owls in an effort to reduce or eliminate local populations and troublesome individual owls. As a youngster in Pennsylvania, I tried to earn extra money by shooting a few of these birds. The instructions in the manual for would-be owl hunters were crisp and clear: Choose a site that afforded a good view of the edge of a woodland while simultaneously providing cover within a patch of brush. Call the Great Horned Owl just at twilight. If it responds but doesn't come within view, retreat 100 feet or so and call again. Better yet, have someone else call from farther away while you remain to survey the woodland edge where the owl is most likely to appear. To obtain the $5 bounty, mail the feet and talons to the state office. For several weeks one cold November, I took up a position that afforded a good view of the woodland edge and tried hooting, squawking, and other assorted calls, mostly mouselike squeaking, that I thought might entice an owl. Somewhat to my surprise, my efforts were rewarded when one of these big creatures landed among the barren branches of a dead elm.

The owl hooted and looked about curiously, no doubt searching for the "other owl" that had intruded into its territory. One good look at this magnificent creature was enough for me; my resolve vanished, and I put my rifle away in the closet, where it remains forty years later.

It took many years before the value of Great Horned Owls was at last recognized, and still more years of dedicated conservation efforts before the bounty on these birds was eliminated—often in stages—in most states and provinces. In Saskatchewan, for example, the year-round open season on Great Horned Owls was first reduced to a five-month period, from November 1 to March 31, in 1960. Only later was the killing of this magnificent owl finally banned altogether, except for individual owls taking poultry.

WANTED ALIVE
BIRDS OF PREY

IT IS A CRIME TO SHOOT <u>ANY</u> BIRD OF PREY

If you find an injured hawk or owl, or want
more information about raptors, contact:

THE RAPTOR TRUST

**1390 WHITE BRIDGE ROAD
MILLINGTON, NJ 07946**

Protection efforts initially were encouraged following recognition that these owls and other birds of prey are biologically beneficial, ecologically important, and environmentally sensitive species that are fully deserving of our protection. By 1970, Great Horned Owls were finally protected everywhere in North America. It is now illegal to trap, shoot, poison, or otherwise molest these owls. The Great Horned Owl is also protected throughout much of Latin America, although there, as in North America, many are still inadvertently trapped or illegally shot for sport.

The protection of Great Horned Owls probably did much to enhance the ultimate population recovery of this owl throughout much of North America. Conservation programs on the part of individuals, environmental organizations, and state and federal agencies have also contributed to the bird's recovery. Other than education programs, most conservation efforts have focused on raptor populations in general rather than specifically on the Great Horned Owl, but it has certainly benefited from these programs.

Goals and efforts of raptor conservation efforts on many wildlife refuges, national heritage sites, national forests, parks, Bureau of Land Management (BLM) lands, and other federal and state lands have involved the protection of nest sites, the establishment of buffer zones around nesting areas or specific nest sites, and the construction of nest boxes or nesting platforms, especially in treeless areas such as the Great Plains or in shrub-steppe habitats.

Great Horned Owl populations are continuing to increase in abundance and distribution throughout much of North America, and the bird is widespread over much of its former range throughout North America, although its numbers are low and thinly spread out. The most recent North American Breeding Bird Survey results show sizable population gains in the Canadian maritime provinces, including Nova Scotia, Prince Edward Island, and Quebec, but significant decreases in Manitoba, Saskatchewan, and the Boreal Plains ecozones.

In the United States, numbers have increased in Utah, the Lexington Plains, Glaciated Missouri Flat, and across much of Central and Southern California, but have declined slightly in most of the Gulf Coast states, Wyoming, and the southern Rockies. None of the Great Horned Owl subspecies are state or federally listed, and this owl is not considered endangered, threatened, or of special concern in most states, although it is included in CITES (Committee on International Trade in Endangered Species of Wild Fauna and Flora) to ensure its protected status.

State and federal agencies continue to track the status of the Great Horned Owl and other bird species across North America by means of Christmas Bird Counts and Summer Breeding Bird Counts. On the local level, both funded and unfunded research by individuals also contributes valuable information about the distribution and ecology of this owl. However, most of the information gathered is somewhat limited and these data are mostly indirect indicators of the bird's population status, because its nocturnal activities and habit of roosting and nesting in concealed locations during daylight hours prohibit any kind of exact count.

The recovery of the Great Horned Owl in some parts of North America has resulted in some rather unusual conservation problems. In the Pacific Northwest, for example, the Northern Spotted Owl *(Strix occidentalis caurina)* is threatened by loss of old-growth forest habitat due to logging and forest fragmentation. The clear-cut and forest edge habitats created by logging provide suitable habitat for an expanding Great Horned Owl population, which preys on spotted owl nestlings and recently fledged young. The combination of habitat loss and increased predation is hampering efforts to save this spotted owl subspecies.

The Great Horned Owl's appetite and hunting prowess have also hampered recovery efforts of other endangered species, notably the Peregrine Falcon, Osprey, and Whooping Crane. At several sites along the East Coast, expensive efforts to raise and return peregrines to the wild from hacking towers were ruined by Great Horned Owls taking the young. This behavior has led to renewed requests to trap and remove the troublesome individuals, which are merely responding to their hunting instincts.

Although most Great Horned Owl populations are sufficiently robust at the present time, this big owl remains vulnerable to human modifications of its habitat and its lifestyle. The Great Horned Owl must be considered always at risk because it is relatively long-lived, occupies the top of the community food chain, occurs in low densities throughout its range, and has a relatively slow reproductive rate. All these factors contribute to its vulnerability in the face of change, particularly human alterations to the landscape.

Despite the conservation efforts, humans remain the cause of most Great Horned Owl deaths in the wild throughout its range. In most cases where the cause of death has been determined, the owls were shot, caught in traps set for game animals, or hit by vehicles.

This last is responsible for the largest number of deaths, possibly because Great Horned Owls tend to fly along and over roadways in search of prey and are blinded by the headlights of oncoming cars. Other human-related causes of death include electrocution by power lines or transmission lines, poisoning, becoming entangled in barbed-wire fences, colliding with structures, becoming trapped in buildings, being caught by dogs, or being struck by trains.

Years of federal and state protection have failed to prevent causal and opportunistic shooting and killing of individuals by sportsmen and "plinkers" armed with rifles or shotguns, bows and arrows, or slingshots. The Great Horned Owl's habits of being active in late evening and early morning and using high, open, conspicuous perches for territorial advertisement or hunting increase its visibility and its risk of falling victim to hunters and shooters who prefer live target practice.

Each year, a few Great Horned Owls are also collected for museum specimens (legally) and taken for the taxidermy trade (illegally). The last is probably less common in North America but perhaps more common in other parts of its range, where it is not protected or where protection measures are only weakly enforced. A few individuals are still taken for zoos, although most specimens held captive are injured birds unable to survive in the wild. Some become pets or may be used for falconry purposes by falconers who prefer variety in their stable of birds of prey. Continued efforts aimed at environmental education at all levels seem to be increasingly successful, however, and the removal rate of Great Horned Owls from the wild for these purposes continues to decline.

That the protective programs and educational efforts are working seems to be indicated by the remarkable recovery of the Great Horned Owl in many parts of its range, coupled with its spread as a nesting species in close proximity to human habitation and human activity, especially in agricultural areas, but also increasingly in a variety of urban and suburban habitats. All of this suggests that the population is growing and expanding, and is quite possibly becoming more tolerant of human-modified habitats. Nevertheless, in spite of the recent population growth, the Great Horned Owl continues to face additional risks from humans in the form of pesticide use and toxic industrial wastes, as well as habitat destruction and fragmentation.

Because of their position at the top of food chains, Great Horned Owls tend to accumulate toxic substances such as pesticides and heavy metals. As an owl takes more and more contaminated prey, it accumulates pesticides in its tissues in a process called biological magnification. Eventually the levels may affect basic physiology, alter behavior, and ultimately prove lethal to the Great Horned Owl.

As with many other birds of prey, these owls are especially susceptible to concentrations of chlorinated hydrocarbons such as DDT and its derivatives, dieldrin, mirex, and PCBs. One study of Great Horned Owl carcasses submitted for analysis between 1982 and 1986 revealed that 5.1 percent were organochlorine pesticide-caused deaths. Other Great Horned Owl carcasses analyzed revealed high levels of PCBs in brain and body tissue.

These owls are also susceptible to secondary poisoning from applications aimed at reducing pest populations. For example, anticoagulant rodenticides used to reduce rodent populations, strychnine-treated grain for eradicating rock doves, and mercury contaminations have all been recorded in tissue samples from Great Horned Owls. The elimination of most of these pesticides from general use has reduced their hazards to Great Horned Owls, although secondary poisonings and accumulations of wastes from pollution sources remain an unknown and unresolved problem.

Since they need relatively large home ranges and sizable prey populations, Great Horned Owls, like other large predators, are highly susceptible to habitat loss and modification. In some areas, these owls have responded positively to changes in the landscape; in other locales, habitat alterations have led to a decrease in numbers; and in still other places changes have irreversibly eliminated both habitat and owl populations.

Unlike many species of wildlife, Great Horned Owls have responded positively to logging in the Pacific Northwest and the fragmentation of substantial portions of the New England forest. The resulting mix of woodland and open habitat has increased certain prey populations while retaining sufficient timbered areas for nesting and roosting purposes.

Urban sprawl seems to pose the greatest threat to the greatest number of Great Horned Owl populations. Even in the middle of the desert, the potential for urban development remains high. Urban sprawl and the quick growth of suburban communities, the spread of housing into rural areas, even the increased emphasis on hiking and other fitness activities all work in ways small or large to the detriment of local owl populations. The conversion of a woodland or wildland habitat into a housing development proves fatal for the Great Horned Owl and almost all other wildlife as well.

Successive depletion of remaining natural landscapes in these areas eliminates both prey and predator populations. Thirty years ago, I could depend on finding a pair of Great Horned Owls every mile or two among the hills and canyons of my central Utah study area in the eastern Great Basin Desert. Today that same area is cut and crisscrossed with dirt-bike and ATV trails. Each weekend, and sometimes during the week, a horde of adventurers from Salt Lake City and Provo descends on this once pristine habitat. They bike, ride, hike, jog, camp, and ultimately invade every canyon and valley that once held nesting populations of Great Horned Owls, Golden Eagles, Ferruginous Hawks, and other raptor species. The sagebrush valleys that once held natural prey populations on which these raptor populations depended are now covered with farms that may forever alter the abundance and diversity of available prey. Farther east, in the morning shadow of the Lake Mountains, houses, gardens, and roadways now mingle in a swelling suburban development built among a pinyon-juniper biome that once held another sizable Great Horned Owl population in central Utah.

The advances—or, perhaps more correctly, the inroads—of a growing civilization will undoubtedly continue well into this century. As a result, it seems probable that there will be a slow but steady retreat of Great Horned Owls from many areas, and eventually a general decline in this great owl's population over much of settled North America. Nevertheless, even this may eventually prove less of a threat than once thought, given the ever-increasing observations of Great Horned Owls nesting, foraging, and roosting in urban and suburban areas.

Given the combination of protective legislation, conservation efforts, and environmental education, the Great Horned Owl has made what appears to be a very successful recovery. After far too many years of persecution, these owls have finally achieved recognition as valuable members of the ecosystems they inhabit. Though they may not be appreciated by all their cohabitants, especially by the animals that serve as their food, this large owl is an integral part of its domain. The apparent stability of the Great Horned Owl population over much of its range, coupled with an increased emphasis on the protection of this species, gives hope that this huge and formidable owl may remain a part of our natural landscape and national wildlife heritage for years to come.

Glossary

Altricial—having young that are blind, naked, and helpless or nearly helpless when hatched.

Asynchronous—used to describe eggs of a clutch being laid at irregular intervals, or the staggered hatching of eggs, which results in a nest of different-aged young.

Branching—activity of young owls as they begin to leave the nest and start to walk around on branches near the nest.

Cere—the skin or horny covering over the first part of the upper mandible. The nostrils are in front of the cere.

Courtship—all behaviors related to pair-bonding of males and females, including communications, flights, advertisements, and other behaviors. Courtship may also be extended to include pair-bonding behaviors and communications that maintain pairs and lead to copulation and fertilization.

Crepuscular—activity during the twilight hours of dawn and dusk. Depending on ecological circumstances, Great Horned Owls may be strictly nocturnal, active only at night, partly diurnal, active during early morning or late evening, or crepuscular.

Dispersal—movement of young away from the nest site following the period of fledgling dependency on adults. Dispersal may be multidirectional and unpredictable. It may also refer to movements of adults out of areas or regions in which prey populations have declined.

Ear tufts—erect or semierect tufts or clumps of feathers that extend upward from the top of the head, giving the appearance of a pair of ears. Ear tufts are not part of the hearing apparatus, but instead probably function in species recognition and species-specific behaviors.

Extirpation—the loss or removal of a species from part of its range. Extirpation is not the same as extinction, which is the total loss of the species.

Fledging—the period of the nesting cycle during which the young leave the nest and learn how to fly. A young bird that has recently gained the ability to fly is called a fledlging.

Fledgling success—an estimate of the number of hatched young that will successfully fledge.

Fovea—area of the retina that has an exceptionally dense concentration of light-sensitive cells. This area is exceptionally dense in owls, providing them with good eyesight at night.

Fratricide—the killing and eating of the younger and weaker nestlings by their siblings.

Gape—the distance across the mouth at the bottom of the open bill. This can also refer to the skin associated with the open mouth.

Hatching success—an estimate of the amount of eggs in one group that will hatch successfully.

Home range—geographic area used by an individual, a pair, or a family unit. Daily and seasonal activities all take place within this area.

Juvenile—the period in the life of a young owl between the growth of the first flight feathers and when fledging takes place, sometimes expanding to include the immediate post-fledging period when the young owls remain in company with the adults.

Molt—the collective shedding and replacement of feathers.

Nesting success—an estimate of the number of nests that will successfully hatch one or more young.

Nestling—a young bird that is still in the nest. The nestling period is the time from hatching to fledging. Owls have a shorter fledgling period than other birds, because the young leave the nest before they are able to fly.

Nominate—the named race, i.e., the race on which the species *Bubo virginianus* was first named.

Owl pellets—compacted packets of undigested prey, which are regurgitated after a meal. The pellets of Great Horned Owls help ecologists determine their food habits.

Pair-bond—a semipermanent relationship established between female and male for breeding purposes.

Postfledging—the period when young are able to fly about but are usually accompanied by their parents, which keep watch over the young, teaching them how to hunt and avoid enemies.

Proteolytic—relating to digestive enzymes that fragment certain proteins.

Raptor—a predatory bird that has sharp, strong talons and a pointed, curved bill. Raptors typically include the hawks, eagles, and falcons. Most American ornithologists also prefer to include the rapacious owls as raptors.

Talons—sharp, pointed claws of raptorial birds.

Territory—the defended part of an owl's home range. An area that is consistently controlled or defended against others of the same species or from other species. These territories contain resources as well as nesting and feeding areas. Territorial behaviors refer to all behaviors related to the establishment, advertisement, and defense of a given area.

The American Subspecies of Great Horned Owls

Bubo—a genus of large owls, all with prominent ear tufts. Globally widespread and found on every continent except Australia and Antarctica. The dozen or so Old World species of *Bubo* are known as eagle owls, in reference to their size and power. They are a widespread and ecologically successful group, occurring in many different habitats of Eurasia and Africa. In the New World, the genus is represented by a single species, the Great Horned Owl *(Bubo virginianus)*.

Bubo virginianus—scientific name of the Great Horned Owl. The genus name, *Bubo*, is Latin for a horned or hooting owl. The name may also derive from the Greek *buzo,* which means "to hoot," or their name *buas,* for a horned owl. The species name, *virginianus,* is the Latin form of Virginia, in reference to the type locality of this species (the place in which the species was first recognized and named).

Bubo virginianus virginianus (Gmelin). The nominate race of the Great Horned Owl. It has an extensive range from Minnesota into southern Canada, along the Great Lakes east to Nova Scotia and the Atlantic seaboard; west to eastern Nebraska, eastern Missouri, and eastern Oklahoma; south to Florida and the Gulf Coast into Texas. This subspecies occupies mostly deciduous and mixed woodland habitats of the eastern United States. It is darker and more brownish, with distinct blackish brown bars, tawny feet, and black barring of feathers.

B. v. subarcticus (Hoy). This subspecies name is a reference to the subarctic (as opposed to high arctic) region it occupies. The range of this northern race extends from the Mackenzie River Valley to central-eastern British Columbia; eastward through Alberta, Saskatchewan, and Manitoba and into northern Ontario; and southward into Montana, Wyoming, and North Dakota. In low food years, this race may wander widely southward. It possibly grades into or shows intermediates with *B. v. lagophonus* and *B. v. pallescens,* which greatly extend its range throughout much of the interior western United States and Canada. The earlier subspecies, *B. v. wapacuthu* (Gmelin), often thought to occupy much of the Canadian area west of Hudson Bay, has now been discredited, while *B. v. occidentalis* is considered by some to be a synonym for *subarcticus.* This race is noted for its comparative paleness, with almost white to buff face and feet and often indistinct ventral barring.

B. v. scalariventris (Snyder). This subspecies is thought by many owl taxonomists to be a variant of *subarcticus.* Its range is northern and western Ontario, and into Manitoba. The Latin *scalari* ("scaly") and *veneris* ("belly") are a reference to the ladderlike color scaling about the breast and belly.

B. v. heterocnemis (Oberholser). A northern subspecies whose range includes northern Quebec, Labrador, and Newfoundland. It may also wander southward in winter. The subspecies name is from the Greek *heteros* ("different") and *cnem* ("leg" or "legging") and refers to the color banding about the feathered legs. This subspecies is a darker gray-brown, with heavy dusky barring on the breast and belly.

B. v. occidentalis (Stone). The range of this subspecies encompasses much of the mountain provinces and states and the Great Basin area, from southern Alberta, Saskatchewan, and Manitoba south through Montana, most of Idaho, Colorado, Nevada, and Utah, to northeastern California, and east into Isle Royale, North and South Dakota, Nebraska, and central Kansas. *Occidentalis* is Latin for "western," a reference to its range. It may possibly integrate with other subspecies, and some owl biologists consider *occidentalis* to be synonymous with *B. v. subarcticus.*

B. v. algistus (Oberholser). Probably the northernmost subspecies of Great Horned Owl, it has a western range, mostly maritime Alaska, possibly extending into interior Alaska somewhat. Its name is from the Latin *algero,* "to be cold." Like *B. v. subarcticus,* this northern subspecies is pale with lighter barring.

B. v. lagophonus (Oberholser). The range of this subspecies is from interior Alaska and Yukon south in mountains or at higher elevations through much of British Columbia and into northeastern Oregon and northwestern Montana. In winter, it may move southward as far as Texas. Its name, from the Greek *lagos* ("hare" or "rabbit") and *phonos* ("killer"), is in reference to its reputation as a hunter of jackrabbits, which are a staple prey species throughout much of its range. Its basic color is an overall gray-tawny.

B. v. saturatus (Ridgway). This subspecies' range extends from coastal southeastern Alaska south through British Columbia, Washington, and Oregon, and along the coast of Northern California. Its name is from the Latin *saturatus,* meaning "a full, rich color," in reference to its darker gray and heavily barred coloration.

B. v. pacificus (Cassin). This subspecies of the Pacific ranges mostly down through California and into northern Baja, possibly just extending into southwestern Arizona. Its name is in reference to its locality along the Pacific coast. This subspecies is an overall darker tawny, with intermediate barring.

B. v. pallescens (Stone). This subspecies ranges from the San Joaquin Valley of California and the deserts of southeastern California and Nevada eastward across southern Utah and Colorado; into western Kansas and north-central Texas; and southward through Arizona and New Mexico into the Sonoran and Chihuahuan states to northern Tamaulipas and western Veracruz of Mexico. Noted for its smaller size and paler coloration with indistinct barring, it is named for its paler or lighter color, the Latin meaning "becoming pale."

B. v. elachistus (Brewster). This subspecies occurs in Baja California, mostly along the southern half of the peninsula. This smaller, somewhat lighter colored owl is named from the Greek *elachistos* ("small").

B. v. mayensis (Nelson). Named for the Maya Indians, this subspecies mostly occupies the Mayan Peninsula, ranging down through much of Central America from Jalisco, San Luis Potosi, and southern Tamaulipas in Mexico south to western Panama. It is noted as a small and short-winged race. The subspecies *mesembrinus* (Oberholser), occurring from the isthmus of Tehuantepec to western Panama, is sometimes included in *B. v. mayensis* and sometimes accorded separate subspecies status.

B. v. nigrescens (Berlepsch). This Latin American subspecies ranges across much of the arid and semiarid puna of the Andes, from Colombia into Ecuador and northwestern Peru. This is the darkest subspecies, with dark, coarse barring and mottling on the upper breast and back. *B. v. colombianus* is probably synonymous with this subspecies.

B. v. deserti (Reiser). This subspecies of arid and semiarid habitats is probably synonymous with *nacurutu.* It has been recorded only from Bahia, Brazil. It is mostly grayish with white-edged upper ear coverts.

B. v. nacurutu (Vieillot). This is probably the most wide-ranging of Latin American subspecies, occurring east of the Andes, although it undoubtedly extends into the Andean foothills, from Venezuela, Guyana, and Peru through Bolivia and southward to central Argentina and Uruguay. It is absent from much of Amazonia. Two other forms, *scotinus* and *elatus,* have now been grouped with this subspecies.

B. v. magellanicus (Gmelin). This mostly southern Latin American subspecies occurs from central Peru southward through Argentina, Chile, Patagonia, and Tierra del Fuego. It is a smaller subspecies with smaller and weaker talons, small bill and ear tufts, and different vocalizations. The song consists of two deep hoots, followed by a low, purring sounding somewhat like *bu-hoohworrrr.* This subspecies has recently been elevated to species status by many taxonomists on the basis of its song (see Konig et al., 1999).

Selected References

Adamcik, R. S., A. W. Todd, and L. B. Keith. 1978. Demographic and dietary responses of Great Horned Owls during a showshoe hare cycle. *Canadian Field-Naturalist* 92:156–66.

Austing, G. R., and J. B. Holt, Jr. 1966. *The World of the Great Horned Owl.* Philadelphia: Lippincott.

Baumgartner, F. M. 1938. Courtship and nesting of the Great Horned Owl. *Wilson Bull* 50:274–85.

——. 1939. Territory and population in the Great Horned Owl. *Auk* 56:274–82.

Bent, A. C. 1938. Life histories of North American birds of prey. Part 2. Owls. *U.S. National Museum Bulletin,* no. 170, 1–482. Reprinted by Dover Publications, New York.
    Although somewhat dated now, as all of the information was compiled prior to 1938, the year of publication, Bent exhaustively summarized all of the available reports of ecology, behavior, and food of North American owls. It is still an excellent source of anecdotal information and one of the first volumes that owl researchers review prior to embarking on their own journeys of discovery.

Clark, R. J., D. G. Smith, and L. Kelso. 1978. *Working Bibliography of Owls of the World.* National Wildlife Federation Scientific and Technical Series, no. 1. Washington, DC: National Wildlife Federation.
    All the books, papers, articles, and news about owls ever published, up to 1978, are presented in this bibliography, which also includes summaries of owl taxonomy and distributional status across the globe. Clark et al. also published an updated summary of owl literature below.

——. 1987. Distributional status and literature of northern forest owls. Pp. 47–55 in *Biology and Conservation of Northern Forest Owls.* U.S. Dept. of Agri. Forest Service Technical Report RM-142. Fort Collins, CO: Rocky Mountain Forest and Range Experiment Station.

Craighead, J. J., and F. C. Craighead, Jr. 1956. *Hawks, Owls and Wildlife.* Harrisburg, PA: Stackpole Company and Wildlife Management Institute. (Reprinted by Dover Publications, New York, in 1969.)

Del Hoyo, Josep, Andrew Elliott, and Jordi Sargatal, eds. 1999. *Handbook of the Birds of the World.* Vol. 5. *Barn-Owls to Hummingbirds.* Bird Life International. Barcelona, Spain: Lynx Editions.
    A stunningly illustrated "tour de force" of all of the world's owls. Photos and plates make this massive, oversize volume a "must see" for anyone even remotely interested in owls. Lengthy and learned introductory chapters precede the section on Barn and Bay Owls of the world, and another equally impressive chapter introduces the typical owls. What makes this volume exceptional is that each species account is by noted field researchers, most of whom have actually conducted research on the particular species.

Earhart, C. M., and N. K. Johnson. 1970. Sex, dimorphism and food habits of North American owls. *Condor* 72:251–64.

Errington, Paul L. 1932. Food habits of southern Wisconsin raptors. Part 1. Owls. *Condor* 34:176–86.

———. 1932. Studies on the behavior of the Great Horned Owl. *Wilson Bull* 44:212–20.

Errington, Paul L., F. Hamerstrom, and F. N. Hamerstrom, Jr. 1940. The Great Horned Owl and its prey in north-central United States. *Iowa Agricultural Experiment Station Research Bulletin* 277:758–850.

Hoffmeister, D. F., and H. W. Setzer. 1947. The postnatal development of two broods of Great Horned Owls *(Bubo virginianus). University of Kansas Public Museum of Natural History* 1:157–73.

   This study, along with Sumner's 1928 study (see below), provides important information about the development of Great Horned Owl young.

Houston, C. S., D. G. Smith, and C. Rohner. 1998. The Great Horned Owl. In *The Birds of North America.* No. 372., edited by A. Poole and F. Gill. Philadelphia: Academy of Natural Sciences; Washington, DC: American Ornithologists' Union.

   Scientific summary of all research about this extremely important species. Emphasis is on ecology, natural history, and behavior of North American subspecies. The reference list includes all-important journal references for this species. C. Stuart Houston has authored an impressive number of research articles on almost all aspects of the ecology of Great Horned Owls in Canada.

Johnsgard, Paul A. 1988. *The Owls of North America.* Washington, DC: Smithsonian Institution Press.

   Interesting and entertaining descriptive summaries of the Great Horned Owl and all the other owls of North America. The detailed accounts are written in an authoritative and entertaining manner. Natural history and ecology are emphasized throughout. This thorough treatment includes a glossary, key to owls, and related materials. This book provides valuable and readable material that permits a comparison of Great Horned Owls with other North American owls.

Konig, C., F. Weick, and J. Becking. 1999. *Owls. A Guide to the Owls of the World.* New Haven, CT: Yale University Press.

   An excellent summary of the taxonomy, distribution, and ecology of all of the world's owls. Well illustrated by Friedhelm Weick.

McGillivray, W. Bruce. 1989. Geographic variation in size and reverse size dimorphism of the Great Horned Owl in North America. *Condor* 91:777–86.

McInvaille, W. B., Jr., and L. B. Keith. 1974. Predator-prey relations and breeding biology of the Great Horned Owl and Red-tailed Hawk in central Alberta. *Canadian Field-Naturalist* 88:1–20.

Petersen, L. 1979. Ecology of Great Horned Owls and Red-tailed Hawks in southeastern Wisconsin. *Wisc. Dept. Nat. Resour. Tech. Bull* 111:1–63.

   Petersen used radiotelemetry to elucidate movements and behaviors of Great Horned Owls in Wisconsin woodland habitats.

Smith, D. G. 1969. Nesting ecology of the Great Horned Owl, *Bubo virginianus. Brigham Young University Biological Series Science Bull* 10(4):16–25.

   This and the next listing are two of a dozen papers and monographs that summarize my studies on the ecology, habitat selection, and nesting of Great Horned Owls in the Great Basin Desert of central Utah.

Smith, D. G., and J. R. Murphy. 1973. Breeding ecology of raptorial birds in the eastern Great Basin Desert of Utah. *Brigham Young University Biological Series Science Bull* 18:1–76.

Stewart, P. A. 1969. Movements, population fluctuations and mortality among Great Horned Owls. *Wilson Bull* 81:155–62.

    One of several studies published by Paul Stewart detailing movements and mortality of Great Horned Owls in North America.

Sumner, E. L., Jr. 1928. Notes on the development of young screech owls. *Condor* 30:333–38.

———. 1934. The behavior of some young raptorial birds. *University California Publications in Zoology* 40:331–62.

Voous, K. H. 1988. *Owls of the Northern Hemisphere.* Cambridge, MA: MIT Press.

Photo Credits

Page 62
Robert McCaw

Page 63
George Robbins Photo

Page 64
Ron Austing

Page 65
Wayne Lynch (top)
Bill Duyck (bottom)

Page 66
Wayne Lynch

Page 67
Richard Day/Daybreak
  Imagery (top)
Ron Austing (bottom)

Page 68
Leonard Lee Rue III

Page 69
Robert McCaw (left)
Richard Day/Daybreak
  Imagery (right)

Page 70
Ron Austing

Page 71
Ron Austing

Page 72
David Dvorak Jr. (top)
Ron Austing (bottom)

Page 73
David Dvorak Jr.

Page 74
Ron Austing

Page 75
Ron Austing

Page 77
Richard Day/Daybreak
  Imagery

Page 78
David Dvorak Jr. (left)
Leonard Lee Rue III
  (right)

Page 79
David Dvorak Jr.

Page 80
Robert McCaw

Page 81
Tom J. Ulrich

Page 83
Wayne Lynch

Page 84
Wayne Lynch

Page 85
Richard Day/Daybreak
  Imagery

Page 86
David Dvorak Jr.

Page 87
Len Rue Jr.

Page 88
Robert McCaw

Page 89
Maslowski Photo

Page 90
Richard Day/Daybreak
  Imagery

About the Author

Dwight Glenn Smith received his introduction to the study of Great Horned Owls and other birds of prey while working with the late Dr. Joseph R. Murphy of Brigham Young University. He has since continued his studies of the ecology of animals—primarily birds of prey—throughout much of North America, Siberia, parts of Africa, and South America. He has published several hundred articles on avian ecology and other science topics; this is his fourteenth book. He is currently professor and chairman of the biology department at Southern Connecticut State University in New Haven, Connecticut, where he has taught botany, zoology, ecology, and mammalogy for more than thirty years.

Index